Western Main Lines

EXETER TO NEWTON ABBOT
via Dawlish

Vic Mitchell and Keith Smith

MP Middleton Press

Cover: Accelerating away from Teignmouth on 19th July 1956 is BR 4-6-2 no. 70023 **Venus** *with the 7.30am Penzance to Liverpool train. The returning holidaymakers are about to have their final trip along the Devon coastline, as the locomotive leans over on the curve leading to the famous sea wall line. (R.C.Riley)*

First published August 2000

ISBN 1 901706 49 4

© Middleton Press, 2000

Design Deborah Esher

Published by
> *Middleton Press*
> *Easebourne Lane*
> *Midhurst, West Sussex*
> *GU29 9AZ*
Tel: 01730 813169
Fax: 01730 812601

Printed & bound by Biddles Ltd,
> *Guildford and Kings Lynn*

CONTENTS

ACKNOWLEDGEMENTS

We are very grateful for the help received from so many of the photographers. Our thanks also go to W.R.Burton, R.M.Casserley, G.Croughton, N.Langridge, Mr D. and Dr S.Salter, G.T.V.Stacey, M.Turvey, E.Youldon and as always, our wives.

GEOGRAPHICAL SETTING

The first eleven miles and the final five are on the level Alluvium of the estuaries of the Rivers Exe and Teign respectively. The intervening four miles are on or in Red Sandstone, most of the route being constructed at the foot of the cliffs on the foreshore. This has proved to be a costly mistake, as marine

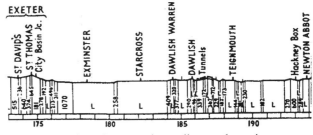

erosion has necessitated continual defensive work and storms have disrupted services on many occasions. Cliff falls have been an added problem. The maps are to the scale of 25 ins to 1 mile and have north at the top.

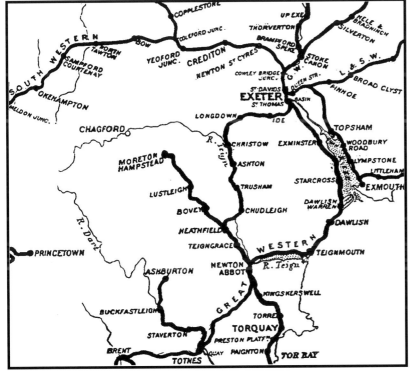

I. The Railway Clearing House diagram of 1917 shows both routes between Exeter and Newton Abbot.

HISTORICAL BACKGROUND

The Plymouth, Devonport & Exeter Railway Company was formed in 1840 to promote a line between those places. Its name was changed to the South Devon Railway in 1843, after Mr I.K.Brunel had been appointed engineer. The Act for its construction was passed on 4th July 1844; the Bristol & Exeter Railway had opened on 1st May of the same year.

Double track was proposed, but this was changed to a single broad gauge (7ft 0¼ ins) line after it was decided to adopt atmospheric propulsion instead of using steam locomotives. The route between Exeter and Teignmouth opened on 30th May 1846, but steam haulage had to be used initially. The line was extended to Newton Abbot on 30th December following and to Totnes on 20th July 1847. The atmospheric system was employed exclusively from 23rd February 1848 but was abandoned totally on 20th September of that year. It was never used west of Newton Abbot.

All 12 goods sidings on the route were privately owned (by Mr. G. Hennet) initially, although on SDR land. Most were available for public traffic, which was often conveyed in one of Hennet's wagons, until his bankruptcy in 1853.

The route mileage west of Newton Abbot increased from 39 to 109 during 1859, the resulting growth in traffic necessitating track doubling thus: Exminster - Starcross in September 1860, Exeter St. Thomas - Exminster in June 1861, Exeter St. Davids - St. Thomas in September 1861, Teignmouth Old Quay to Newton Abbot Teign Bridge in July 1865 and the section from the bridge to the station in the following October.

A short goods branch to the Exeter Canal Basin was opened on 17th June 1867, but it was connected only to the down line. A third rail was available from 1876 for traf[fic] to and from the standard gauge London & South Weste[rn] Railway, which had reached Exeter St. Davids on 1st Fe[b]ruary 1862.

Double track between Starcross and Dawlish w[as] brought into use on 16th February 1874; betwe[en] Teignmouth Station and Old Quay on 25th May 1884 a[nd] between that station and Parson's tunnel (west of Dawlis[h]) on 6th July 1884.

The SDR became part of the Great Western Ra[il]way on 1st February 1876 and conversion of the route [to] standard gauge took place on 21-22 May 1892. The [re]maining single line section near Dawlish had five tunne[ls] and was thus the most expensive to widen. Work started [in] 1901 and the double track was opened in two stages [to] 1905.

Thus one of Brunel's errors of judgement had at la[st] been overcome. His enthusiasm for the inadequately prove[n] atmospheric system had been another costly mistake. Su[b]sequent generations of railway engineers and operators hav[e] had to deal with the absurdity of building a railway at th[e] foot of storm-lashed cliffs. Despite his bad advice to th[e] GWR regarding gauge and the use of longitudinal sleepe[rs] (of necessity perpetuated on the SDR), he is ranked as on[e] of the greatest engineers of his age. The alternative inlan[d] route was in use from 1903 to 1958 and was often used f[or] diversions during inclement weather.

The subject of this album became part of the Wes[t]ern Region of British Railways upon nationalisation [in] 1948. Privatisation resulted in Great Western Trains ope[r]ating services from Paddington from 4th February 199[7] with Virgin Cross Country, Wales & West and South We[st] Trains soon running other services on the route.

ATMOSPHERIC TRAINS

The concept of a series of lineside vacuum pumps to evacuate a tube between the rails to provide a means of train haulage had been successfully employed on the Kingstown & Dalkley Railway (near Dublin) since March 1844. A piston in the pipe was connected to the leading vehicle through a slot, which was covered by a leather flap to act as a valve. A similar system was used between Croydon and New Cross from January 1846 to May 1847 and is shown in diagrams III and IV in our *London Bridge to East Croydon* album. Intended to run between London and Epsom, the line's stations were sited at the summit of short inclines, so that trains could gravitate to the commencement of the pipe. On the SDR, the initial momentum was provided by a rope connected to a piston in a short auxiliary trackside vacuum pipe, but often the station staff had to assist with their shoulders.

The 15 ins diameter pipes commenced outside each station and were fitted with valves at each end, these being worked by trips. There were eight pumping stations in which boilers had to be maintained at working pressure for about 20 in every 24 hours. The associated engines were designed to work the vacuum pumps for 5 to 8 minutes prior to the passage of a train and for a similar time during its journey. The durations were much longer in practice, owing to leak[-]age at the longitudinal valve. The leather deteriorated du[e] to the effects of flexing, frost, vacuum, salt and the variou[s] sealing compounds applied by gangs of "greasers" whic[h] proved of limited value. The job was dangerous due to th[e] speed and silence of the trains; 40 mph was common an[d] 70 mph was not unknown. The blowing of a horn was th[e] only safety measure available. The braking was errati[c], trains often overrunning the stations sometimes to the e[x]tent of entering the next pipe and being whisked off to th[e] next "stop". Shunting at each end of the route was unde[r]taken by locomotives or manually, the latter being a com[m]on practice at that time.

The system had the advantages of lower fuel cost[s], no smoke or smut nuisance, steady and quiet running pl[us] the impossibility of head-on or rear-end collision outsid[e] the stations.

Inexplicably, Brunel failed to extend the electric te[l]egraph system to the engine houses and so there was [a] great amount of unnecessary and wasteful pumping un[der]taken. This fact, combined with the many other prob[lems], resulted in the cessation of atmospheric working o[n] 10th September 1848, just after a new rubber valve ha[d] arrived for installation.

1.   Jacob and Joseph Samuda's Patent specification included this diagram in which the piston carriage bodywork was omitted. These vehicles were never turned, as the connection to the piston was at an angle. At the points, there were slopes between the rails known as "piston inclines", which forced the piston up to clear the rail that it was crossing.

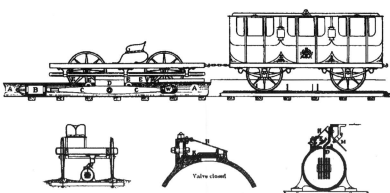

A.	Continuous pipe fixed between the rails	F.	Roller attached to carriage for closing the valve
B.	Piston	H.	Weather valve
C.	Iron plates connected to the piston	K.	Continuous airtight valve
D.	Plate connecting apparatus to carriage	M.	Roller attached to carriage for opening weather valve
E.	Metal rollers to open the continuous valve	W.	Counterweight to piston

2.   The only known illustration of a piston carriage is incomplete and is on the edge of a watercolour. The part to the right of the right axle is conjectural. There is no record of the title given to the man in charge. He was hardly a driver - he had no control over the propelling force, only an indication of its power from a lineside vacuum gauge. His skill

was in applying the brakes. Trains of five coaches would travel at about 50 mph in favourable conditions; the problem was stopping! (W.Dawson)

3.   To improve performance west of Newton Abbot it was decided to replace the 15 ins diameter pipes with ones of 22 ins. However, the system was abandoned before they were installed. A few served as a drain on Goodrington Beach, until moved to the Didcot Railway Centre where they have been laid on a length of broad gauge track. The engine houses were at Exeter, Countess Wear, Turf Level Crossing, Starcross, Dawlish, Teignmouth, Summer House and Newton Abbot.
(V.Mitchell)

DIVERSIONS

II.   The 1946 map (right) is at slightly less than 1 ins to 1 mile and omits the urban areas at each end of the route, but includes the GWR ferry between Starcross and Exmouth. A £3m scheme was prepared in 1936 for a line between Exminster and Bishopsteignton to avoid the unsatisfactory coastal route. It is superimposed hereon, as is the shorter 1937 route, starting near Dawlish Warren. Three short tunnels plus one of 2624 yds, were proposed. The ruling gradient was 1 in 150, slight compared with the climb west of Newton Abbot, much of which is around 1 in 50. (Brunel intended that route also for atmospheric working. He could have chosen one of the alignments marked or the Heathfield route, which involved little tunnelling, when constructed). The effects of the impending war meant that the scheme was suspended and the land purchased was sold, mostly around 1949. The only work on the ground that had been undertaken involved land clearance and marking out. No announcement was made regarding possible stations on the diversion, but it was assumed that the coast route would have remained open for local traffic.

PASSENGER SERVICES

Down trains running on most days of the week are considered in these notes. The initial timetable showed seven trains, this dropping to six when services were extended to Newton Abbot. However, a timetable produced during the brief period of atmospheric working indicated ten departures from Exeter, but the 3.0pm terminated at Teignmouth.

Extreme economy was necessary after the financial disaster brought on by the atmospheric failure and only five trains were operated. There was a gradual improvement between 1852 and 1858, by which time eight trains were run each weekday, a figure that was maintained for about a decade.

Although through running of a few trains between London and Plymouth began in 1850, most day trains were locals and stopped at all stations between Exeter and Newton Abbot until 1890. A sleeping car service began in 1877, by which time there were eleven trains along the route.

A supplementary local service was introduced in 1905, using railmotors. Originating at Exeter St. Thomas, there were two trips to Teignmouth and three to Dawlish. Some journeys were extended to Torquay in 1909 and, from 1912, the unit was based at Newton Abbot from where it did two trips to St. Thomas and two short workings. They mostly ceased during World War I.

Dawlish and Teignmouth have normally had a similar number of stopping trains, although in the 1920s and 30s there were usually a few more at the latter place. For most of the 20th century the number has been 20 to 25, although it increased in the 1930s. It was 27 in December 1935, for example, with three more in the Summer. These figures include railmotors, which reappeared in 1924, the year in which extra trains on Saturdays were first introduced for holidaymakers.

World War II brought further cutbacks, the railmotors vanishing for ever and the two main stations having only about 15 trains each day. The lesser stations suffered more drastic cuts. While there were some improvements, notably in the 1950s, there were further cuts in 1966-68. Sleeping car trains ceased to make stops on the route in 1977.

A notable improvement was effected in 1982, when one up local train was extended to Exeter Central, the closest station to the city centre. More followed in later years, all continuing to Exmouth. The local frequency returned to about 25 trains on weekdays.

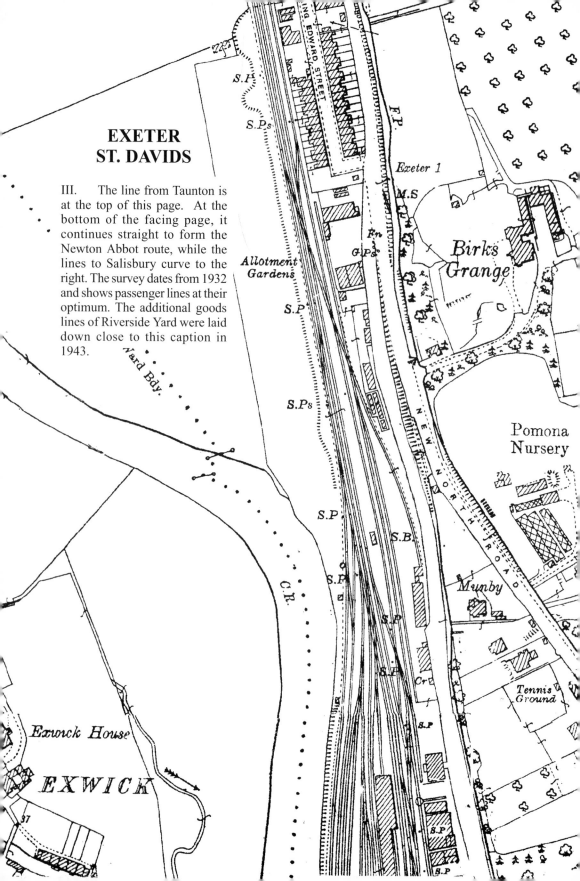

EXETER
ST. DAVIDS

III.   The line from Taunton is
at the top of this page. At the
bottom of the facing page, it
continues straight to form the
Newton Abbot route, while the
lines to Salisbury curve to the
right. The survey dates from 1932
and shows passenger lines at their
optimum. The additional goods
lines of Riverside Yard were laid
down close to this caption in
1943.

Allotment
Gardens

S.P

S.Ps

S.P

S.P

S.P

S.B.

S.P

Munby

Cr

S.P

Yard Bdy.

C.R.

Exwick House

EXWICK

37

KING EDWARD STREET

F.P.

Exeter 1

M.S

Fn
G.Ps

Birks
Grange

NEW NORTH ROAD

Pomona
Nursery

Tennis
Ground

S.P

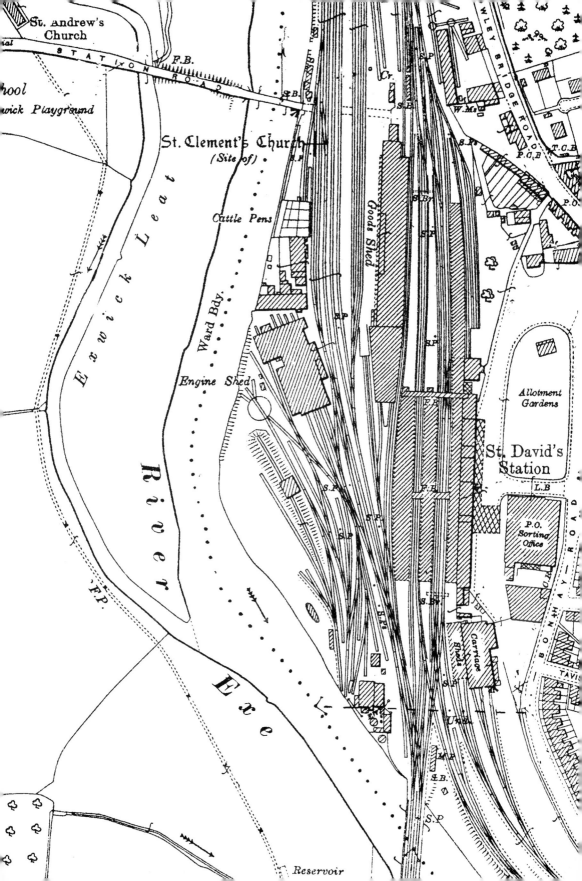

St. Andrew's
Church

St. Clement's Church
(Site of)

Cattle Pens

Exwick Leat

Ward Bdy.

Engine Shed

River

Exe

F.P.

Goods Shed

S.P.

St. David's
Station

Allotment
Gardens

L.B.

P.O.
Sorting
Office

Carriage
Shed

S.B.

S.P.

Reservoir

STATION ROAD

F.B.

S.B.

Cr.

W.Ms.

P.O.B

T.C.B

P.O.

hool
wick Playground

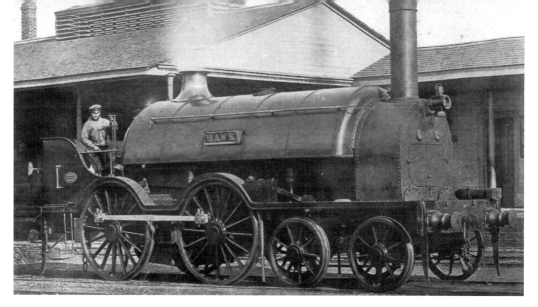

4.　　Like many of the original GWR through stations, St. Davids had a single long through platform, with a crossover near its mid-point and a roof over adjacent tracks. Only the latter can be seen in this view; it had been built by the BER. *Hawk* was originally a SDR locomotive, having been built by Slaughter Grunning in Bristol in 1859. It was withdrawn in December 1885 as GWR no. 2108. (M. Dart coll.)

6. The 1860 facade, with its ornamental urns, was retained during the rebuilding 50 or so years later. It was photographed on 28th February 1928 as the Corporation's Car 6 was about to climb back to the city centre. The system, which is illustrated in the Middleton Press *Exeter and Taunton Tramways*, closed in 1931. (BR/R.M.Casserley coll.)

5. The second station had four platforms, with a single overall roof, and was erected during the 1860s. It was replaced in 1911-14 by the one illustrated in this southward view, recorded in 1921. It had five through platforms, plus the bay on the left. The towers house the luggage lifts and the roof on the right is that of the goods shed. Goods traffic ceased on 27th February 1978. (LGRP/NRM)

7.   Viewed from a train departing southwards on 31st August 1945 is no. 6016 *King Edward V*, which is on the bridge over the River Exe. The first structure here had been the property of the SDR, while the station was owned by the BER. This is the third bridge and it dates from 1896. (H.C.Casserley)

9.   The transition to diesel traction began in 1958 with the introduction of the D600s. Seen on 28th May 1962 is no. D822, with the "Torbay Express" bound for Kingswear. (T.Heavyside)

8.   Rising above all else is the facade from the 1860s and on the right is the former broad gauge carriage shed. Recorded at the head of the "Royal Duchy" on 19th July 1958 is 4-6-0 no. 6839 *Hewell Grange* and 4700 class 2-8-0 no. 4701. The perforated signal arms were used for backing moves. (R.C.Riley)

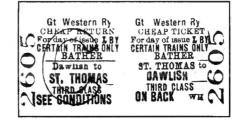

1924

10. As a result of flooding, the up "Royal Duchy Express" was diverted to run via Exeter Central, Salisbury and Basingstoke. It awaits an SR engine, while a WR 0-6-0 pannier tank keeps the steam heating going on 27th October 1960. (D.Edmund/ S.P.Derek coll.)

→

11. The evening sun forms a shadow of part of no. 6827 *Llanfrechfa Grange* as it departs with the 3.50pm Bristol Pylle Hill to Plymouth parcels train. Through freight trains usually used the adjacent track. This picture was taken on 23rd June 1962, as was the next. (R.C.Riley)

→

12. Turning about 90 degrees, the photographer recorded the lower part of the curved 1 in 37 incline to Exeter Central, the Exe flood plain, no. 4993 *Dalton Hall* shunting empty coaches and Exeter West Box. (R.C.Riley)

13.   During the Winter timetable in GWR days, it was the usual practice to divide some Paddington-Plymouth trains at Exeter St.Davids, with the rear portion forming a stopping service thence to serve intermediate stations to Newton Abbot and Kingswear. This practice was continued by BR into the late 1960s and here, on 31st December 1968, Class 22 no. D6310 waits with the Paignton portion (including the restaurant car) off the 12.30 Paddington - Plymouth. (G.Gillham)

14.   With West Box behind the third coach, no. 50038 (later named *Formidable*) departs south with the 16.30 Paddington to Paignton on 2nd July 1975. The signal gantry was replaced by the one seen in the next picture on 23rd November 1975. (D.H.Mitchell)

15.   HSTs were introduced to the route in the 1980-81 timetable; this example was recorded working from Penzance to London on 25th April 1983. West Box remained in use until 17th November 1986 and was subsequently dismantled and rebuilt at the Crewe "Railway Age". (T.Heavyside)

16.   Following the failure of no. 47567 while working the 12.12 mail train from Penzance to Glasgow on 3rd May 1991, no. 50018 was provided to assist. They are crossing the Exe bridge, which was replaced in October 1997. (D.H.Mitchell)

17.   Running over Red Cow Level Crossing on 16th March 1994 is a class 159 DMU. This type operates regularly between Waterloo and this station, but a few trips are extended to Paignton. It is seen from the north end of platform 3 and is running from the carriage sidings in the background into platform 1. No. 2 is the bay platform on the right. (M.J.Stretton)

Other Middleton Press albums featuring Exeter:
Branch Lines to Exmouth
Branch Line to Moretonhampstead
Exeter to Barnstaple
Exeter to Tavistock
Yeovil to Exeter

18.   Viewed from the south end of platform 6 in 1998 is the Exeter Area Signalling Centre. It opened on 29th March 1985 and extended its activity beyond Exeter to Hackney Yard, near Newton Abbot, in November 1986 and to include Newton Abbot in May 1987. West Box stood close to this site until 1913. (P.G.Barnes)

EXETER ST. DAVIDS ENGINE SHED

19.   A northward view includes the four-road 1894 shed and the turntable road running diagonally across its tracks. The two unoccupied lines at the lower border of the picture are the through goods lines, which were in use until 27th February 1978. (BR)

20.   The reroofed shed was photographed in May 1962 with 0-6-0PT no. 9480 nearest. We list the 1947 allocation and in brackets are the 1962 figures, by which time there were three diesel shunters as well. Six 4-6-0s (13), three 4-4-0s (0), three 2-8-0s (0), four 2-6-0s (3), three 2-6-2Ts (3), nine 0-6-0PTs (9) and five 0-4-2Ts (6). (S.C.Nash)

21.   The shed roof had been removed by the time that this photograph was taken on 23rd June 1963, closure being effected on 14th October of that year. The inclined road to the coal stage is on the left. The original broad gauge shed had been to the left of this view. (C.L.Caddy)

22.   The 76,000 gallon water tank had just been removed from the top of this building when it was photographed in March 1982. It had started life as an atmospheric pump house and was later used for producing gas for carriage lighting and dining car cookers. Photos 11, 12 and 19 were taken from its windows. (D.H.Mitchell)

23.   The site was used for diesel stabling and as a fuelling point. It was recorded on 30th May 1991. Five tracks sufficed and on the nearest is no. 50003 *Temeraire* in Network SouthEast livery. Next is no. 50050, repainted in its original guise as D400, and on the right is no. 50031 *Hood*. The last diesel shunter (no. 08792) left in September 1999. (G.Gillham)

24.   Although giving an appearance of great antiquity, all the structures seen here from the south in this 1921 view date from 1861, when the track was doubled. The first small and inadequate station was improved in 1847 by the addition of a wooden ground level building and a trainshed over part of the single platform. There was a curious irritant for travellers until 1862; up trains called to set down only. (LGRP/NRM)

25.   The trainshed is viewed from the north in 1959, when the generous facilities were still complete. Being closer to the city centre and western suburbs, the station had been well used in earlier years. Unlike the other stations on the route, it had no gap in the atmospheric pipe and so trains often overshot the platform, as they had to be braked against the propulsion force. (Stations UK)

IV.   The 1932 survey has the station top left and the 1903 Alphington Road Goods Depot lower right. An elevated coal siding was added in 1851 on the site of the building shown at an angle to the main line (top left corner). The siding was in use until 1884 and the site continued to serve as a coal yard until 1930, when a railwaymen's club was erected on it.

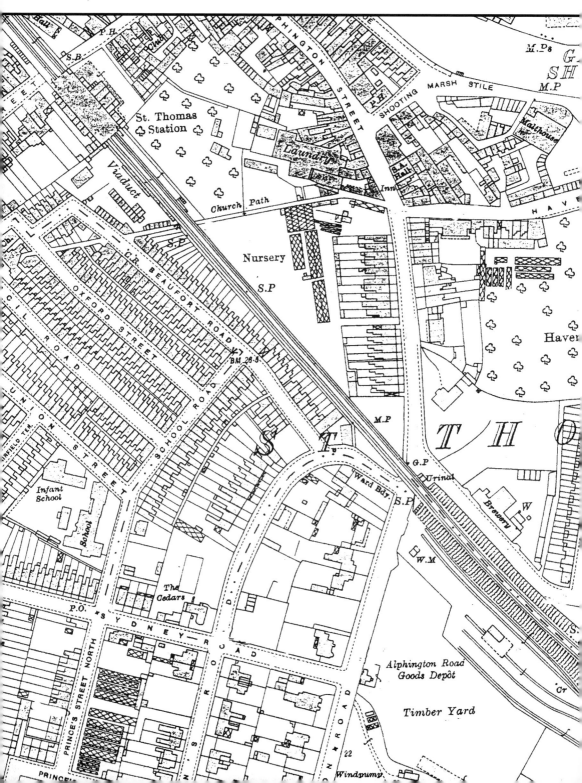

26. The 1861 building was photographed in 1959. There was a signal box to the right of this southward view from 1867 to 1959. A short trailing siding was added near it for stabling terminating railmotors in 1905. It was lifted in 1949. The temporary buildings were for traders displaced by road widening. (S.P.Derek)

27. No. 47446 passes through with a train bound for Paignton, staffing having ceased in 1971. Down stopping trains had dropped from 14 in 1959 to 7 in 1968, but rose to 15 in 1988. The overall roof had been demolished in 1970. This photograph was taken on 14th May 1979, as was the next. (T.Heavyside)

28. The line in this vicinity was laid on a 548yd-long viaduct which carried it over the three roads radiating west from the city. Level crossings were not desirable on an atmospheric railway. "Bubblecar" no. 55025 and a 2-car DMU pass over the 1861 arches as they approach the up platform. In the distance is Exeter City Basin signal box, which closed on 17th November 1986. (T.Heavyside)

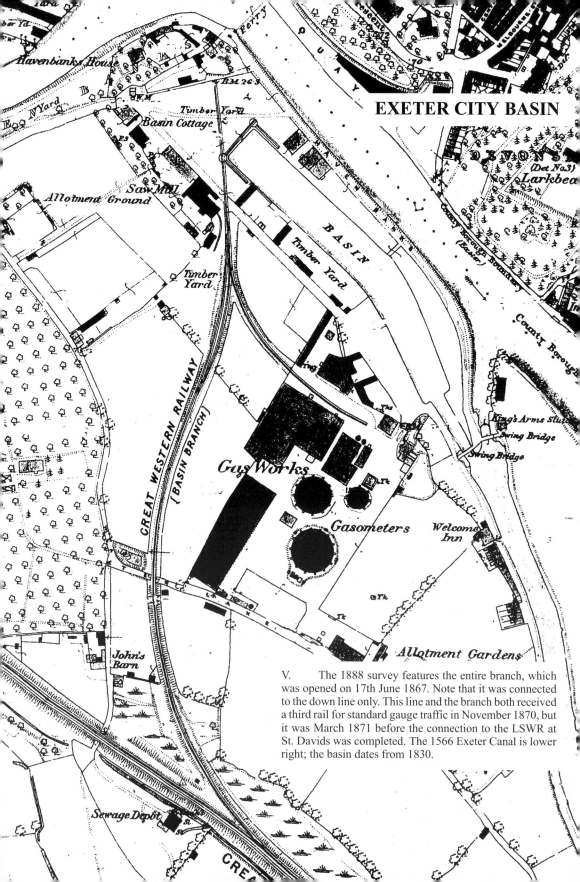

EXETER CITY BASIN

Havenbanks House

N Yard

Timber Yard

Basin Cottage

Saw Mill

Allotment Ground

Timber Yard

BASIN

Timber Yard

DEVON (Det No 3) Larkbea

County Borough Boundary (Exeter)

County Borough

GREAT WESTERN RAILWAY (BASIN BRANCH)

King's Arms Stable

Swing Bridge

Swing Bridge

Gas Works

Gasometers

Welcome Inn

John's Barn

Allotment Gardens

V.　The 1888 survey features the entire branch, which was opened on 17th June 1867. Note that it was connected to the down line only. This line and the branch both received a third rail for standard gauge traffic in November 1870, but it was March 1871 before the connection to the LSWR at St. Davids was completed. The 1566 Exeter Canal is lower right; the basin dates from 1830.

Sewage Depot

CRE

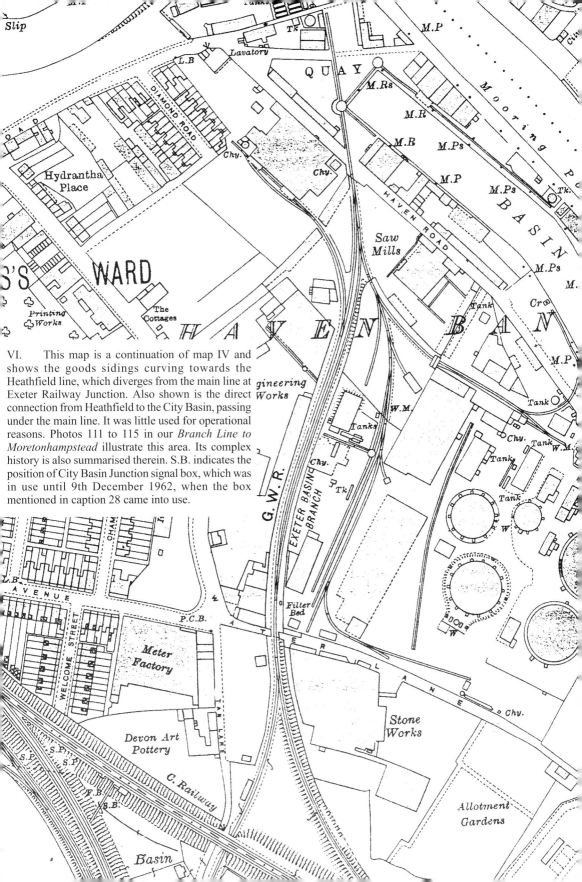

Slip

Lavatory

QUAY

DIAMOND ROAD

L.B.

Chy.

Chy.

Hydrantha
Place

Saw
Mills

HAVEN ROAD

WARD

Printing
Works

The
Cottages

H A V E N

B A N

M.P

M.Rs

M.R

M.R

M.Ps

M.P

M.Ps

BASIN

Mooring Po

Tk.

M.Ps

M.

Cr

M.P.

Tank

Tank

Chy.

Tank

W.M.

Tank

VI.   This map is a continuation of map IV and
shows the goods sidings curving towards the
Heathfield line, which diverges from the main line at
Exeter Railway Junction. Also shown is the direct
connection from Heathfield to the City Basin, passing
under the main line. It was little used for operational
reasons. Photos 111 to 115 in our *Branch Line to
Moretonhampstead* illustrate this area. Its complex
history is also summarised therein. S.B. indicates the
position of City Basin Junction signal box, which was
in use until 9th December 1962, when the box
mentioned in caption 28 came into use.

gineering
Works

W.M.

Tanks

Chy.

Tk.

Tank

Tank

W.M.

W

G.W.R.

EXETER BASIN BRANCH

CHAM

CHAM

L.B.

A V E N U E

WELCOME STREET

TAN LANE

P.C.B.

Meter
Factory

Devon Art
Pottery

C. Railway

S.P.

S.P.

S.P.

F.B.

S.B.

Filter
Bed

A   T   E   R   L   A   N   E

Stone
Works

Chy.

Allotment
Gardens

Basin

EXMINSTER

29.   Not only did George Hennet own the goods facilities, as elsewhere on the route, but he unusually provided passenger accommodation here as well. This came into use in August 1852, by which time the SDR was financially exhausted. It had recovered sufficiently to buy the station in January 1857, following Hennet's bankruptcy. A "passing siding" was added in 1859 and a down platform came with the doubling in 1861, as did the road bridge shown. The shelter on the right was built in 1869. (Lens of Sutton)

VII.   This map was published in 1939 and includes the platform steps, the roadside booking office and the pumphouse (right).

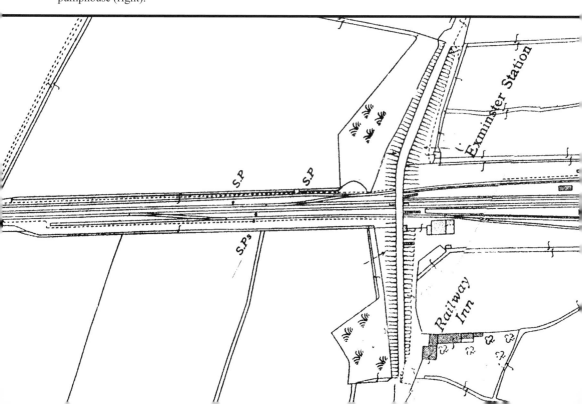

30.   The service of down trains was thus: 2 in 1850s, 4 in 1860s, 5 in 1870s and 80s, 6 or 7 in 1890s and 9 by 1903. A peak of 19 called in 1905, 13 in 1913, fewer in World War I, a high of 14 in the mid 1930s, followed by a steady decline. This southward view is from 1921 and includes the 1911 extension to the 1852 building; it lasted only 20 years. Hennet's coal shed is near the water tower. A urinal was erected beyond the down platform shelter at the time of the gauge conversion in 1892. The signal box had 14 levers when built in 1893. The goods connection from the up line was removed in 1924, leaving only the 1921 link from the down line. Beyond it is the cattle pen and beyond that is the pump house. (LGRP/NRM)

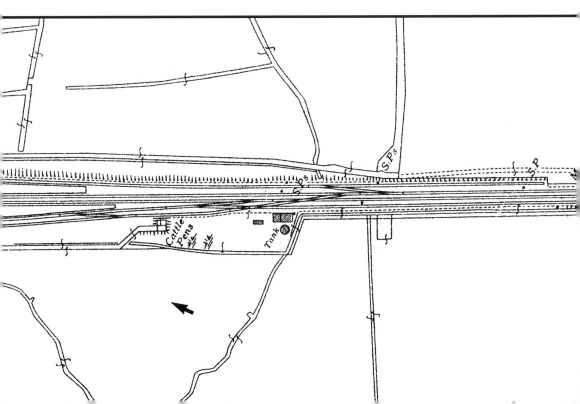

31. Extensive alterations were made in 1931 to provide quadruple track through the station. New features included two additional bridge spans, four platform faces, new shelters and a larger water tank, unusually near the middle of the platform. A new goods siding was laid in the form of a loop. The centre bridge span was replaced in 1929 and again in 1970. (LGRP/NRM)

32. A 1963 northward view includes the signal box, which opened on 9th June 1924 when the down loop came into use. Another line was laid behind it in 1941, it leading to three sidings south of the station. These were intended for holding wartime trains. An additional water tank was erected just behind the cameraman at that time. Also the down refuge siding, beyond the bridge, was converted to a goods loop. (C.L.Caddy)

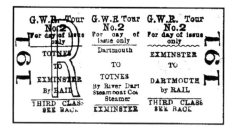

G.W.R. Tour No.2
For day of issue only
TOTNES TO EXMINSTER
By RAIL
THIRD CLASS SEE BACK

G.W.R Tour No.2
For day of issue only
Dartmouth TO TOTNES
By River Dart Steamboat Co.
Steamer
EXMINSTER

G.W.R. Tour No.2
For day of issue only
EXMINSTER TO DARTMOUTH
by RAIL
THIRD CLASS SEE BACK

33.   The sidings referred to in the previous caption were extended south in 1942 to make connection with the down loop. After the war, these additional lines were used mostly for carriage storage, as can be seen here on 23rd June 1963. No. D843 *Sharpshooter* is speeding north with LMR coaches, as wagons stand in the goods yard. (C.L.Caddy)

34.   Closure was thus: to passengers on 30th March 1964, to goods on 6th September 1965 and to coal traffic on 4th December 1967. "Peak" class no. D87 runs north on 27th August 1973, after the platforms had been removed. It is easy to see why the 1911 extension of the station had to be removed for the new up loop in 1931. The trackwork was reduced in stages from 1962, until the 80-lever signal box closed on 17th November 1986. Before the two northern sections of the box were added in 1941, it had 56 levers. The structure was extant in 2000, having been used by bird watchers for a period. (D.H.Mitchell)

35.   With Exeter and the M5 bridge in the background, no. 45016 approaches the station site with the 07.35 Leeds to Penzance on 23rd July 1979. There was a population of 3300 at the time of closure, but the village centre was half a mile distant and it was well served by buses. (D.H.Mitchell)

36.   The building had ceased to serve passengers in 1931, when a small booking office was erected at the west end of the road bridge. No. 47411 is working a Plymouth-Manchester service on 18th December 1982 and is passing the remnant of the up loop, which had been truncated near the rear coach in 1976. After years of dereliction, the old station was converted to a fine dwelling, the site later being used for architectural salvage. (D.H.Mitchell)

SOUTH OF EXMINSTER

37.   The first feature south of the station was the water troughs, which were supplied by the pumphouse mentioned earlier. They were in use from 1904 to 1962. Next was Powderham Signal Box which, like Cotfield to the north of Exminster, opened in 1924. They closed in 1964 only having been in use on Summer Saturdays. (C.L.Caddy)

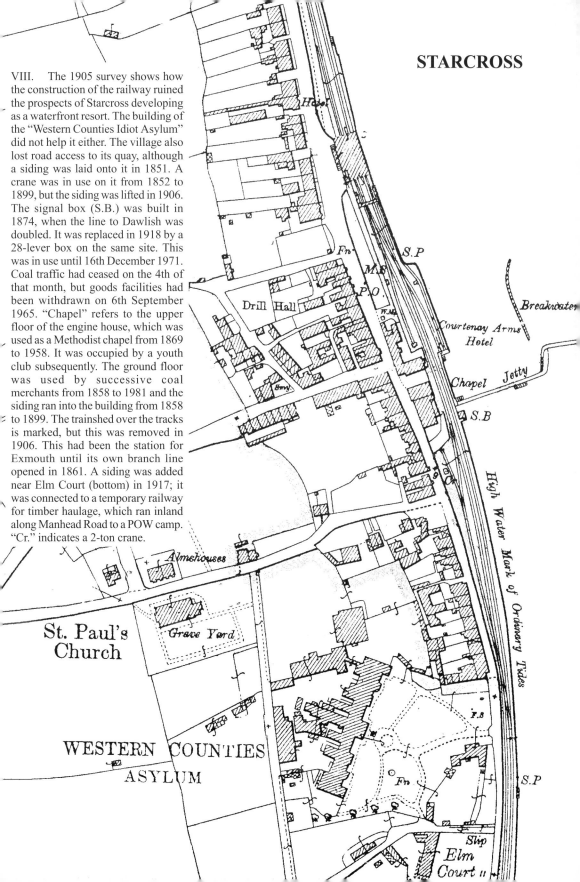

STARCROSS

VIII.   The 1905 survey shows how the construction of the railway ruined the prospects of Starcross developing as a waterfront resort. The building of the "Western Counties Idiot Asylum" did not help it either. The village also lost road access to its quay, although a siding was laid onto it in 1851. A crane was in use on it from 1852 to 1899, but the siding was lifted in 1906. The signal box (S.B.) was built in 1874, when the line to Dawlish was doubled. It was replaced in 1918 by a 28-lever box on the same site. This was in use until 16th December 1971. Coal traffic had ceased on the 4th of that month, but goods facilities had been withdrawn on 6th September 1965. "Chapel" refers to the upper floor of the engine house, which was used as a Methodist chapel from 1869 to 1958. It was occupied by a youth club subsequently. The ground floor was used by successive coal merchants from 1858 to 1981 and the siding ran into the building from 1858 to 1899. The trainshed over the tracks is marked, but this was removed in 1906. This had been the station for Exmouth until its own branch line opened in 1861. A siding was added near Elm Court (bottom) in 1917; it was connected to a temporary railway for timber haulage, which ran inland along Manhead Road to a POW camp. "Cr." indicates a 2-ton crane.

Hotel

Breakwater

Fn

S.P

M.P

P.O

Drill Hall

Courtenay Arms Hotel

Chapel   Jetty

Smy

S.B

High Water Mark of Ordinary Tides

Almshouses

St. Paul's Church

Grave Yard

WESTERN COUNTIES ASYLUM

Fn

F.8

S.P

Slip

Elm Court

38.   This 1949 northward view features the original "temporary" timber building. The initial platform was on a loop line, the main line being on the site of the present down line. A roof covered part of the platform and the adjacent track. A second platform (only 5ft wide) was built on top of the sea wall in 1848. (LGRP/NRM)

————————▶

39.   A siding was provided for coal for the atmospheric pumping house from the outset and Hennet was allowed to lay one for public traffic close by in 1851. It was acquired by the SDR in 1857 and is seen on 16th July 1955, as no. 6838 *Goodmoor Grange* works an up special train for the staff of Swindon Works. The population was a little over 2000 at this time. (R.C.Riley)

————————▶

40.   No. D1023 *Western Fusilier* roars past the weed covered platform on 29th December 1975, as a Devon General AEC rounds the corner, ready to scoop up any local passengers. Up trains called only at 13.22, 16.22, 16.56 and 17.58 - not very useful. The path to the Exmouth ferry is on the left. The pier and ferry rights had been purchased by the SDR in about 1843 and were sold by BR in 1981. Winter ferry services ceased in October 1966, after rail parcel service had been withdrawn. (C.L.Caddy)

41. No. 50029 *Renown* stops with the 11.05 Paignton to Waterloo Sundays-only train on 1st July 1990. There were 14 up departures on weekdays at this time. In the background is the atmospheric engine house, which was saved from demolition by a listing in 1979. It was purchased privately and opened as a museum of atmospheric propulsion in 1982. It was possible to travel on a small flat wagon, powered remotely by a vacuum cleaner! The building was sold to a sailing club in 1993. (P.G.Barnes)

42. A view from the top of the engine house on 27th June 1992 includes no. 47832 *Tamar* and the 1895 footbridge, which was replaced in December 1999. The track curvature north of the station had been reduced in 1906 and staffing ceased on 3rd May 1971. The Brunelian building was demolished in 1981 and replaced by public toilets at the west end of the footbridge. The only other comfort for passengers was an open shelter on the up platform. (D.H.Mitchell)

SOUTH OF STARCROSS

43.   A rare sighting of steam was to be had at Cockwood Harbour on 2nd May 1994, in connection with the Exeter 150 Railfair. Nos. 80080 and 80079 are in full flight northwards. A pier was built south of this location in 1867-68 and oyster beds were established. The Exe Bight Oyster Fishery & Pier Company was not a success, but some coal was landed there and conveyed from the nearby SDR siding to Exeter Gasworks until about 1878. (D.H.Mitchell)

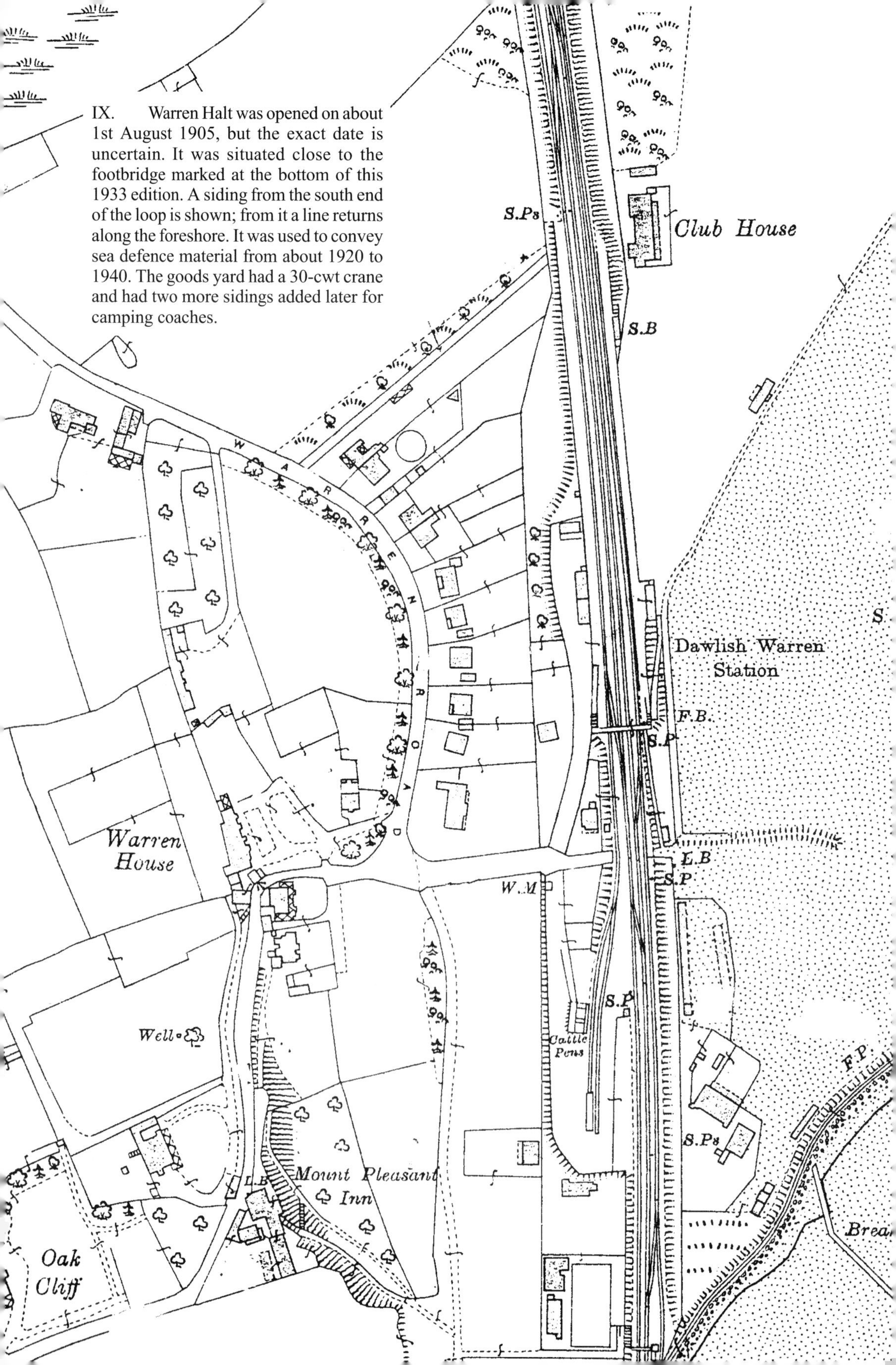

IX.   Warren Halt was opened on about
1st August 1905, but the exact date is
uncertain. It was situated close to the
footbridge marked at the bottom of this
1933 edition. A siding from the south end
of the loop is shown; from it a line returns
along the foreshore. It was used to convey
sea defence material from about 1920 to
1940. The goods yard had a 30-cwt crane
and had two more sidings added later for
camping coaches.

S.Ps

Club House

S.B

W A R R E N

R O A D

Dawlish Warren
Station

S.

F.B.

S.P

Warren
House

L.B
S.P

W.M

Well

S.P

Cattle
Pens

S.P

F.P.

Mount Pleasant
Inn

L.B

S.Ps

Oak
Cliff

Brea

FP

DAWLISH WARREN

44.   Warren Halt had timber framed buildings, one on the up side and two on the down. Teignmouth-bound steam railmotor no. 72 is hauling a clerestory trailer coach and largely obscures the Pagoda shelter. This view is after the platforms had been lengthened in 1906. It was renamed "Warren Platform" on 1st July 1907, when it became staffed. The name was changed again on 1st October 1911, when it became "Dawlish Warren", having been rebuilt slightly further north. (Lens of Sutton)

45.   Beyond the crossover on the left, a train stands on the goods loop. This was available for use by passenger trains from 1942 and the crossover was removed in 1952, creating one long down loop. The up stopping train is hauled by one of the "Saint" class. There was a staff of 5 or 6 in the 1930s. (Lens of Sutton)

46.   A 1921 northward view includes the signal box, which opened on 12th October 1911. The goods yard followed on 10th June 1912, but traffic was always light. This new station came into use on 23rd September 1912. The goods shed seen beyond the main building, was adapted as a waiting room in 1956. The station was closed as a wartime measure from 1st January 1917 until 5th May 1919. (LGRP/NRM)

47.   No. 4145 has come to the end of the down loop on 3rd July 1957 with the 9.20am Taunton to Goodrington Sands stopping train. On the left is a camping coach. The first arrived here in 1935, a 10-berth model, available at £5 per week. They were reintroduced after the war, in 1952, and by 1959 there were nine coaches. (R.C.Riley)

48.   Southern Region locomotives appeared on the route regularly to keep their drivers familiar with the line when used for diversions. No. 34024 *Tamar Valley* is entering the first cutting on 17th June 1958 with the 11.35am Exeter St. Davids to Kingswear. The station is in the background. (S.C.Nash)

49.   A class 47 hauled the 06.45 Saturdays only Worcester to Penzance Motorail service on 26th July 1975. The goods yard ceased to perform its intended function on 5th August 1963 and was used exclusively for camping coaches thereafter. (S.P.Derek)

50.   A westbound HST is seen from the end of the down platform on 25th April 1983. To the left of it is a crossover from the up platform line to the up main. The signal on the extreme left is for the up goods loop. Until 1974, the platforms continued well past the box, which was closed on 14th November 1986. It had 58 levers. (T.Heavyside)

51.   An up DMU keeps to the main line on the same day, while we have an opportunity to examine the mechanical signalling. The connection to the up platform line is on the right. Staffing had ceased in May 1971 and the bridge between platforms was removed in 1977, although it had been renewed in 1964. More recently, there has been a staff presence at busy times. (T.Heavyside)

52.	No. 150269 was recorded working the 11.17 Paignton to Exmouth service on 16th March 1994; it is signalled for the platform line. Note the rock defences on the right. To study the erosion problems, the Soils Mechanics Laboratory of BR set up an anemometer nearby in 1952. BR withdrew from the camping coach business in 1964 and the vehicles passed to the Staff Association. They were replaced by more modern ones in 1982, but there was no longer a rail connection. They are on the left of centre. (M.J.Stretton)

53.	The low winter sun picks out no. 158820 forming the 11.55 Cardiff-Penzance passing on 21st December 1994. The train is running over the facing crossover, installed in November 1986 to allow single-line working (over the up line) between here and Teignmouth at times when storms cause the down line to be threatened by heavy seas. (G.Gillham)

54.	The up side building was still intact when the "Dawlish Donkey" stopped for photography on 12th April 1998. It had been converted to a holiday flat in 1986. The down side had been destroyed by fire on 9th January 1924 and its replacement was demolished in about 1980 in favour of the hut on the right. No. 1450 is an ex-GWR 0-4-2T and is normally based on the East Somerset Railway. The tall structure in the background is a golf ball screen. (P.G.Barnes)

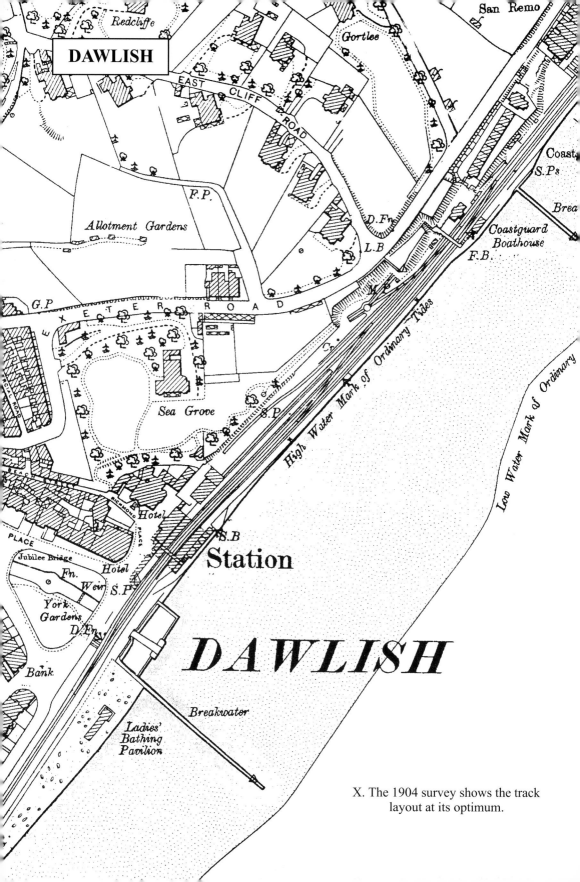

X. The 1904 survey shows the track
layout at its optimum.

55. As at Starcross, there was initially a small timber building, with a trainshed across the solitary platform and one track. The loop received a platform, as shown, in May 1858. In the background is the atmospheric engine house and near the locomotive is the elegant colonnade with Grecian columns, which gave pedestrian access to the beach. (M.J.Dart coll.)

56. This "temporary" building lasted until destroyed by fire in August 1873. A new station had been planned in connection with the 1874 doubling from Starcross. It was completed in April 1875. When the line was proposed, the town recorded a population of 3132 in 1841. (M.J.Dart coll.)

57. A westward view includes the 1879 Boat Cove footbridge and a good example of broad gauge track, the timber transoms being correctly exposed for inspection. Unobtrusive wire fencing was demanded by the residents. (C.J.Clinker coll.)

58.   The track curvature was reduced and a sea wall was built at the time of the doubling westwards in 1905. This further reduced the width of the beach. Few resorts have been so scarred by a railway. (M.J.Dart coll.)

59.   An up railmotor waits under the fully enclosed footbridge in about 1908, as a crowd stands in hope of appearing on a postcard. The vaulted canopy had an unusual cast iron valance. (M.J.Dart coll.)

60.   The atmospheric engine house stood on the right, until demolished in 1868. The goods yard was of limited capacity; the main traffic was coal and the principle user was the gasworks. (Lens of Sutton)

61.   The signal box dates from 9th September 1920, its predecessor having been on the down platform. No. 3383 is working the 4.30pm Paignton to Exeter on 2nd September 1936. There was a staff of 14 between the wars. (K.Nunn/LCGB)

62.   The platforms were lengthened several times, notably in 1875 and 1934. No. 6007 *King William III* races past with the up "Devonian" on 28th August 1937. The goods yard often contained horse boxes for race horses at that time; earlier the GWR had stables nearby. (J.G.Sturt)

63.   A 1949 photograph features the 1937 replacement footbridge, which was only partially enclosed. Both platforms had water columns, the 1907 tank being visible beyond the signal box. There were steps on the right, down to the promenade at beach level, making Dawlish an attractive location for the "Bucket & Spade Brigade". (LGRP/NRM)

64.   Through freight traffic was substantial. Notable in the up direction was fish, vegetables, horticultural products and china clay. One such train was recorded on 8th September 1955, behind ex-WD 2-8-0 no. 90563. (N.L.Browne)

———————▶

65.   The goods yard and its 6-ton crane are visible as no. 7029 *Clun Castle* (now preserved) runs past with "The Devonian" on 5th July 1957. It closed on 17th June 1965. Prone to failure, the cliff face has been partially cement rendered. The goods shed was demolished in 1969. (R.C.Riley)

———————▶

66.   A shortened high speed train of two power cars (rearmost is no. 253017) and two 1st class carriages, approach Kennaway Tunnel while on a crew-training trip between Taunton and Plymouth, prior to the introduction of the West of England HST service in the Autumn of 1979. The date is 27th July 1979. (S.P.Derek)

67.	No. 50026 *Indomitable* hauls the 09.20 Liverpool to Penzance train over the steel spans that replaced the colonnade in 1928. The date is 16th March 1981. The canopy had been replaced in 1961 by a concrete structure with wired glass, but the latter did not withstand the onslaught of the stone-throwing sea. A stream runs between the railings. (D.H.Mitchell)

68.	A class 45 runs between the crowded beach and the packed car park on 24th July 1983. Not only was the station and track attacked by the sea regularly, but signalling problems often resulted from its effects on track circuiting. (P.G.Barnes)

69.	The class 142 "Skipper" units were introduced to the West Country as a replacement for the conventional DMUs in early 1986, but before long it was found that their long rigid wheelbase was unsuitable for the many tightly-curved branch lines in this area and by the end of the following year they had been transferred to the north-east of England.. No. 142020 bounces away from Dawlish station forming the 17.45 Exmouth-Paignton service on 28th August 1987. (G.Gillham)

70.　No. 47515 *Night Mail* is working a daytime train from Paddington to Penzance on 27th May 1989. The up platform was shortened in 1970, but the signal box last worked on 27th September 1986. It had only been used on Summer Saturdays since 1970, with only seven levers working in its 25-lever frame, which was removed in 1989. The box was still standing in 2000. (P.G.Barnes)

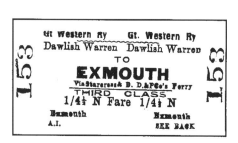

71. . The wall was built in 1901-02 in readiness for the doubling. Despite its presence, the sea breaks over the track regularly in Winter. A more peaceful scene was recorded on 29th September 1991 as no. 50030 *Repulse* avoids the sea wall line as it approaches the 209yd long Kennaway Tunnel with the 12.20 Exeter St. Davids to Paignton. (D.H.Mitchell)

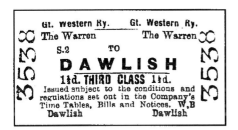

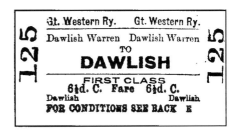

72.   The 07.16 Penzance to Glasgow is about to enter Kennaway Tunnel on 28th June 1990. The double track tunnel came into use on 1st October 1905. The public footbridge replacement dates from 1965 and serves Boat Cove. (P.G.Barnes)

→

73.   Beyond Kennaway Tunnel is Coryton's Cove and the 224yd long Coryton Tunnel. No. 1450 has emerged from it with the "Dawlish Donkey" on 11th April 1998. The 55yd long Phillot Tunnel is to the south. (P.G.Barnes)

74.   Ex-ROD 2-8-0 no. 3014 leaves Coryton Tunnel with a westbound freight in 1936. This tunnel was also enlarged for double track and was ready on 4th June 1905. (M.J.Dart coll.)

——————————▶

75.   Dawlish is in the background as no. 31195 emerges from Clerks Tunnel with an engineers train on 28th August 1987. This was once a favourite location for taking photographs for GWR publicity material. The train will soon pass through Parsons Tunnel which is 521yds long. (G.Gillham)

——————————▶

76.   At Shell Cove, between the two shorter tunnels, a serious wash-out occurred in 1880. It gave a rare view of the timber piles that supported Brunel's baulk road. Their uneven settlement gave his track a bad reputation in some areas, owing to its switchback configuration. The early telegraph system is also evident. (M.J.Dart coll.)

77.   A near disastrous landslip east of Parsons Tunnel happened on 29th December 1852. The transfer of passengers was recorded on canvas early in January 1853. The line was closed for four days. The folly of accepting Brunel's route soon became apparent. The track was attacked by natural forces from both sides on many occasions. To protect the track here, the tunnel was extended eastwards by 147yds in 1920-21. (F.Jones/Rly.Mag.)

78.   Subsequently to be found on the East Somerset Railway, BR class 9F 2-10-0 no. 92203 runs west with vans in the Summer of 1961. Parsons Tunnel Signal Box had six levers, with only four in use. It was open on Summer Saturdays only from 16th April 1947 to 1st April 1964. It had been built in 1934 on the site of a 12-lever box, which had been in use from 1906 to 1911. The 1884 box was nearer the tunnel and closed when the doubling was completed in 1906. (C.L.Caddy coll.)

79.   The end of the sea wall path is seen in this and the previous picture. Walkers pass under the track and turn inland at this point, up Smugglers Lane. No. 47242 is passing a mound of defensive rocks on 23rd June 1976 with a smart train of Mk I coaches forming the 07.40 Penzance to Liverpool. (G.Gillham)

80. A little further west, no. 4966 *Shakenhurst Hall* passes Parsons Tunnel down home signal on 28th August 1936. The train was noted as being the 9.50am Saltash to Exeter St. Davids. The angle of the near cliff face had been reduced with much manual effort in the 1920s and drainage was also improved. (K.Nunn/LCGB)

81. Seen at the same location on 26th July 1975 is the 17.40 Paignton to Kensington Olympia, which ran on Summer Saturdays only. The train could be used by non-motorists as far as Ealing Broadway, where it arrived at 21.07. Road improvements and increasing charges brought Motorail services to an end. A renaissance in 1999 was unsuccessful. Sprey Point is in the background. (S.P.Derek)

82. Trains pass in the same vicinity on 3rd September 1955. Nearest is no. 1011 *County of Chester*. A scenic joy in Summer, Brunel's over optimism has been cursed by frustrated engineers and delayed passengers in Winter, particularly in 1846, 1853, 1855, 1859, 1869 and 1872. Massive expenditure subsequently has reduced the frequency of blockage, but not sea water problems. (N.L.Browne)

EAST OF TEIGNMOUTH

83. This is the same location as the cover picture, but before 1884, when work of eliminating Eastcliff Tunnel was completed. Difficult to discern are the points to Eastcliff Loop, which was in use from 1852 to 1884, when double track linked it to Teignmouth station. It extended in the other direction to Parsons Tunnel. (M.J.Dart coll.)

84.　To reduce the delays due to the malfunctioning of the 1986 track circuiting in high seas, a series of 16 sets of axle counters was installed in March 1990. A computer matches the counts and warns the Exeter signaller of any discrepancies due to beam interruption. No. 50037 has come to the end of the sea wall on 11th May 1979, with a Mk II coach leading. The photographer took the next picture from near the third coach. (T.Heavyside)

85.　The railway has disrupted Christian life in this town. The Wesleyan Methodists had to be provided with a new chapel and burial ground in 1845. Sadly the latter was on Eastcliff and was required for the cutting seen here. Its creation also necessitated demolition of the Catholic church; its 1881 replacement is in the background, but St. Michaels (left) remained untouched. No. 50030 is working from Penzance to Paddington on the same day. Note the World War II gun emplacement. (T.Heavyside)

TEIGNMOUTH

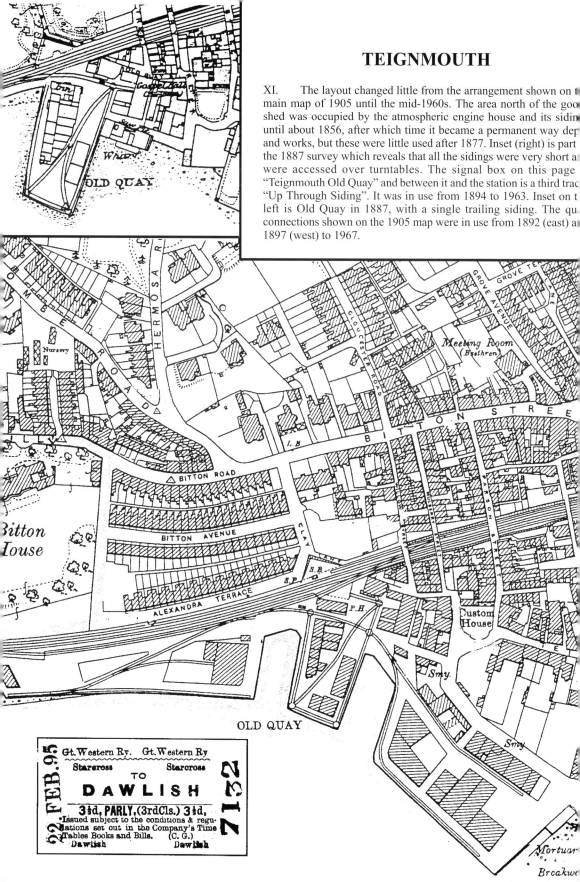

XI.   The layout changed little from the arrangement shown on t...
main map of 1905 until the mid-1960s. The area north of the goo...
shed was occupied by the atmospheric engine house and its sidin...
until about 1856, after which time it became a permanent way dep...
and works, but these were little used after 1877. Inset (right) is part...
the 1887 survey which reveals that all the sidings were very short a...
were accessed over turntables. The signal box on this page...
"Teignmouth Old Quay" and between it and the station is a third trac...
"Up Through Siding". It was in use from 1894 to 1963. Inset on t...
left is Old Quay in 1887, with a single trailing siding. The qu...
connections shown on the 1905 map were in use from 1892 (east) a...
1897 (west) to 1967.

OLD QUAY

OLD QUAY

86.   A westward view from 1893 includes the original platform (left) and trainshed, which spanned two tracks from the outset. The second platform and shed extension date from 1848 and two short canopies were added in 1860. The transverse track ran from the engine shed into the goods shed, which was behind the main building, on the left. The town housed over 4000 souls when the station opened.
(Lens of Sutton)

87.   The original station became very dilapidated and was replaced by a well ornamented stone-built structure in 1894. A similar style had been used a little earlier at Torquay and from Acton to Slough. We look west in this postcard view. (Lens of Sutton)

88.   The goods sidings were completely rearranged during the 1895 rebuilding and Myrtle Road bridge was extended, as seen, to give space for a trailing access to the new yard. This 1921 view shows that gas lights were still in use. Although the station appears to be in a cutting, the entrance is at ground level. The staff was around 30 in the 1930s. (LGRP/NRM)

89.　　The south elevation is pictured in 1955. The GWR had also used this design for a number of late-Victorian buildings in the Midlands. On the left is the gateway to the dock. Coal traffic was low at this station, as much of the domestic requirement arrived by sea. However, coal traffic continued until December 1967. (Lens of Sutton)

90.　　The signal box (right) dates from 1896 and it had 25 levers. It is at the west end of the down platform and was in use until 14th November 1986, although it was closed on Winter Sundays in its final years. The platforms are at their optimum length in this 1956 photograph. (H.C.Casserley)

91.   "The Devonian" was caught in the evening sunshine behind no. 5079 *Lysander*, as it entered the down platform on 13th July 1959. The special short up starting signal was necessary due to the space constraints evident in the next picture. (R.C.Riley)

92.   We have a glimpse of the goods shed in January 1965 and the opportunity of appreciating the sighting difficulties encountered by staff during shunting operations. Goods ceased on 14th June 1965, newspaper traffic in 1988 and Red Star parcels in 1991. The up platform was extended towards the right in 1980-81 to accommodate HSTs. (C.L.Caddy)

93. A smart no. 47455 runs through with the 09.18 Penzance to Leeds on 4th April 1986. Note that the up starting signal had been replaced and repositioned. The down platform had been extended to accommodate 15 coaches in 1938, but the part in the foreground was no longer used, hence the lack of white edging. The station has changed little and was renovated tastefully in 1998. (G.Gillham)

4. A class 50 runs into the station from the west n 11th May 1979. This cutting had accommodated ree tracks until 1968, although the third had only been siding since 1965. It had been on the right, but the emaining lines had been slewed subsequently The rossover was moved 220 yds west in 1981 and has een retained as a companion to the one seen in picture 3, for use in times of high seas. (T.Heavyside)

TEIGNMOUTH OLD QUAY

95.   The Paddington to Newquay service passes over the facing points on 11th July 1956, hauled by no. 7036 *Taunton Castle*. The port had been controlled by the City of Exeter until 1852, but thereafter George Hennet developed the quay, laid sidings and acquired a fleet of 12 ships. An international import and export business developed, greatly benefiting the railway. The end of the third track is on the left. The signal box was in use from 1884 until 9th March 1969; it had a 19-lever frame. (R.C.Riley)

96.   Coal is much in evidence as no. 5999 *Woolaton Hall* works a stopping train from Paignton to Bristol on 17th July 1958. Much of the coal for Newton Abbot power station was landed here after it opened in 1928. The Teignmouth Quay Co. Ltd. had been established in 1886 and it developed Eastern Quay by about 1893 and Western Quay by 1896 (see map XI), either side of Old Quay. In addition to having to change the gauge of its sidings, the company made a number of alterations to the layout of their sidings. (R.C.Riley)

97.   Horses carried out the shunting until the turntables were eliminated in about 1920. An unsuccessful petrol tractor was followed by this 1924 Sentinel in 1931. Fitted with a vertical boiler, *The Elephant* was active until 1963, when it was sold for preservation. It was busy with china clay exports and timber imports for many years and was photographed in 1956. (M.J.Dart coll.)

98.   Old Quay is on the right of this 1955 view of the signal box. The port continues to be busy, although entirely served by road. (P.W.Gray)

Gt. Western Ry   Gt Western Ry
TEIGNMOUTH TEIGNMOUTH
TO
PLYMPTON
THIRD   CLASS
4/3 Fare 4/3
Issued subject to the conditions&regulations set
out in the Company's Time Tables, Bills & Notices
PLYMPTON   PLYMPTON

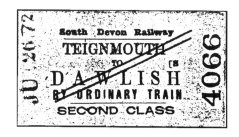

South Devon Railway
TEIGNMOUTH
TO
DAWLISH
BY ORDINARY TRAIN
SECOND CLASS

WEST OF TEIGNMOUTH

99.   West Quay is in the left background as 0-6-0PT no. 1608 works a local freight service towards Newton Abbot on 13th July 1959. There were regular workings between Teignmouth and nearby Hackney Yard. The divergence of the fences from the tracks indicates the greater curvature of the broad gauge tracks. The train is about to pass under Shaldon Bridge, seen in the next picture. (R.C.Riley)

100.   The bridge carries the B3199 across the Teign Estuary as well as over the railway. Behind the camera was the waterside Teignmouth Gasworks of 1840. It was not until 1925 that a short trailing siding was laid. The works were in use until 1956, but the siding was retained until 1960 by a subsequent occupant. No. 25224 heads the 15.30 Exeter to Paignton on 25th June 1976. (G.Gillham)

101.   From a similar viewpoint to picture 99, we see no. 45003 with empty china clay wagons and military vehicles amongst its load on 11th May 1979. It will soon pass the site of Bishopsteington signal boxes which were on the down side and in use in 1909-13 and 1923-69. The second box had eight levers. (T.Heavyside)

EAST OF NEWTON ABBOT

102.   This eastward view from Wolborough Hill in May 1965 has Hackney Yard and its signal box in the middle distance. Between the water tank and the main lines is the 1941 up goods loop, which became a siding in 1971 and was removed in 1981. Hackney Box was at the west end of the diversion proposals in the 1930s. Lower right is the station, East Box and another water tank. (P.W.Gray)

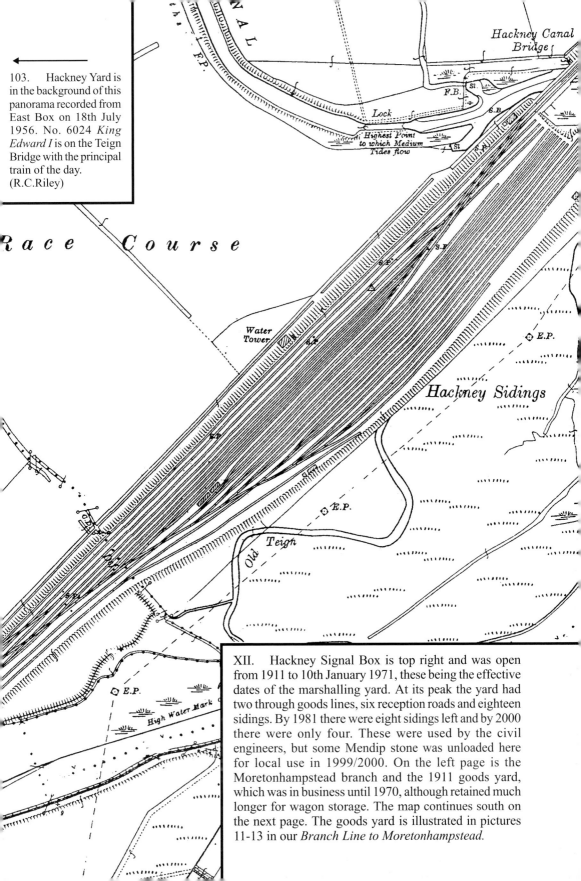

On the map (clockwise from upper right):

Hackney Canal Bridge

F.B.

Lock

Highest Point to which Medium Tides flow

S.B.

E.P.

Hackney Sidings

E.P.

E.P.

Water Tower

Race Course

Old Teigh

E.P.

High Water Mark

103. Hackney Yard is in the background of this panorama recorded from East Box on 18th July 1956. No. 6024 *King Edward I* is on the Teign Bridge with the principal train of the day. (R.C.Riley)

XII. Hackney Signal Box is top right and was open from 1911 to 10th January 1971, these being the effective dates of the marshalling yard. At its peak the yard had two through goods lines, six reception roads and eighteen sidings. By 1981 there were eight sidings left and by 2000 there were only four. These were used by the civil engineers, but some Mendip stone was unloaded here for local use in 1999/2000. On the left page is the Moretonhampstead branch and the 1911 goods yard, which was in business until 1970, although retained much longer for wagon storage. The map continues south on the next page. The goods yard is illustrated in pictures 11-13 in our *Branch Line to Moretonhampstead*.

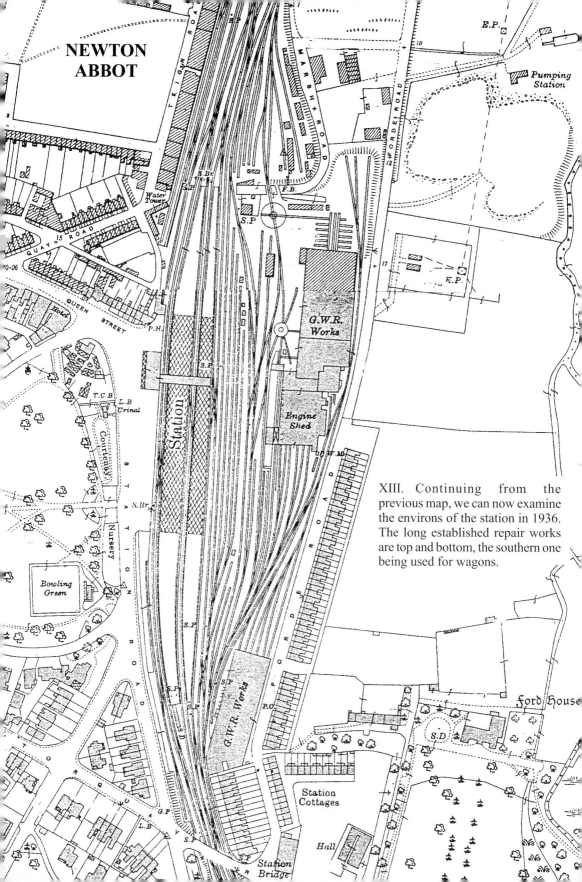

NEWTON ABBOT

XIII. Continuing from the previous map, we can now examine the environs of the station in 1936. The long established repair works are top and bottom, the southern one being used for wagons.

G.W.R. Works

Engine Shed

G.W.R. Works

Station

Bowling Green

Nursery

Courtenay

Pumping Station

Ford House

Station Cottages

Hall

Water Tower

Quay Road

Queen Street

Forde Road

Marsh Road

Teign Road

104.   The first station lasted until 1861 and was succeeded by the one seen here. It had three passenger lines, two having a platform on both sides, so that passengers from main line trains using the outer tracks could easily join a branch train on the centre one. There was a fourth passenger line to the south, for through down trains. The photo is dated 1920. (LGRP/NRM)

105.   Plans for a third station were drawn up in 1908 but various problems delayed its completion until 1927. The exterior is seen in 1923. The old goods shed had been beyond the left border of the picture and was demolished in 1911, after the one shown on map XII had been completed. (Lens of Sutton)

106.   The north end is seen during the demolition. With the gable end removed, it is possible to see the internal footbridge. Summer traffic was increasing greatly and was overwhelming the little station. The next was partially wrecked in August 1940, but that was due to German bombs. (Lens of Sutton)

107.   The new platforms were of generous width and had substantial canopies. SR 2-6-0 no. 1848 was working the 4.35pm Plymouth North Road to Exeter St. Davids on 30th August 1945, its SR crew maintaining their familiarisation of the GWR route. It is standing on the up main, adjacent to the up through. The up relief is on the left, while the carriages on the right are in the Moretonhampstead bay, platform 9. (H.C.Casserley)

108.   The running shed (no. 83A) is seen from the end of the down platform in August 1953. The water column and signal on the left are for trains on the down through line. The six-road shed was completed in 1893 and was provided with a new turntable (65ft long) in 1926. (N.L.Browne)

109.   A closer view of the steam depot in June 1954 includes nos. 4127, 4547 and 5362. It ceased to house locomotives in June 1962, prior to which time the allocation was 26 4-6-0s, 4 2-6-0s, 18 2-6-2Ts, 14 0-6-0PTs, 4 0-4-2Ts and 10 2-8-0s. The corresponding figures in 1947 were 29, 3, 18, 6, 4 and 4. Additionally there was one "Britannia" 4-6-2 in 1962 and nine other locomotives in 1947. (Photomatic)

110.   The Teign Bridge shudders as no. 7824 *Iford Manor* rumbles over it with an Exeter-Paignton service on 15th July 1959. East Box (left) was in use from April 1926 until 1st May 1987. (R.C.Riley)

111.   *Tiny* was a broad gauge relic that could be seen on the down platforms until 1980. The engine was built for the SDR's Sutton Harbour branch by Sara & Co. in 1868 and after withdrawal in 1883 it went to the nearby repair shops as a stationary boiler. It went on display here in 1927 and is now at the museum adjacent to the station at Buckfastleigh. (D.Clayton)

112.	There continued to be a down through passenger line south of the station after the 1925-27 rebuilding. No. 6024 *King Edward I* is using it on 3rd June 1961, as other locomotives stand in the shed yard. (T.Heavyside)

113.	The power station in the background had six sidings from 1928 to 1968, but they were little used in the final years. No. D859 *Vanquisher* takes the up through with coal empties on 9th April 1966. (T.Heavyside)

114. Class 35 no. D7084 runs in with a down train on the same day. The then recently closed inland route to Exeter curves away to the left. The first part (to Heathfield) was still open for china clay traffic at the end of the century. (T.Heavyside)

115. The floodlights of the diesel depot yard are in the background as we have a glimpse of the workshop traverser on 25th September 1971. These lines vanished in about 1978, as the site was partially cleared. The building had been extended in 1924 and was known as the "Locomotive Factory", although it was only used for heavy repairs. (D.H.Mitchell)

116.   The diesel fuelling shelter is on the right and the tanks are visible behind the withdrawn consumers of the oil (nos. 808, 844, 858 and 834) on 15th October 1971. The lines in the foreground lead to four of the five parallel carriage sidings. The wagon works closed in January 1972 and the remaining main line diesels were transferred to Laira Depot. Some class 08 shunters remained until complete closure on 4th October 1981. (T.Heavyside)

117.   No. 50029 *(Renown* from October 1978) departs with up freight (including sheeted china clay) on 1st March 1977. Only three platform faces were used after 1987 and all three lines were signalled for reversible running. No longer did passengers have to climb stairs to reach the two platforms nearest the booking hall. (T.Heavyside)

118. No. 47199 waits with the 19.30 Motorail service to Stirling, while sister locomotive 47063 passes on the up through line with a short train of empty oil tank wagons on 27th June 1976. The track on which it stands was abolished in the May 1987 remodelling, but the bay line was still in place in 2000. (G.Gillham)

119. The fine signal gantry and its wooden posts, all from 1927, were to have a 60-year life. "The Great Western Limited" was part of the GW150 celebrations on 7th July 1985. The locomotives were no. 5051 *Drysllwyn Castle* and no. 4930 *Hagley Hall*. The 205-lever signal box was the largest remaining on the Western Region at that time. (S.P.Derek)

120. The "Dawlish Donkey" was operated during Easter 2000 by BR class 4 2-6-4T no. 80098 and it is seen waiting to return to Exeter at 15.51 on 22nd April. Also evident are remnants of the steam and diesel depots, the former's saw-tooth walls having been listed despite the absence of a roof. Plans were being made for a transport museum. (V.Mitchell)

Other views and maps of this station can be found in our
Branch Line to Moretonhampstead **and**
Branch Line to Kingswear.

MP Middleton Press

Easebourne Lane, Midhurst, W Sussex. GU29 9AZ Tel: 01730 813169 Fax: 01730 812601
If books are not available from your local transport stockist, order direct with cheque,
Visa or Mastercard, post free UK.

BRANCH LINES
Branch Line to Allhallows
Branch Line to Alton
Branch Lines around Ascot
Branch Line to Ashburton
Branch Lines around Bodmin
Branch Line to Bude
Branch Lines around Canterbury
Branch Line around Chard & Yeovil
Branch Lines around Cromer
Branch Lines to East Grinstead
Branch Lines of East London
Branch Lines to Effingham Junction
Branch Lines around Exmouth
Branch Line to Fairford
Branch Lines around Gosport
Branch Line to Hawkhurst
Branch Lines to Horsham
Branch Lines around Huntingdon
Branch Line to Ilfracombe
Branch Line to Kingswear
Branch Lines to Launceston & Princetown
Branch Lines to Longmoor
Branch Line to Looe
Branch Line to Lyme Regis
Branch Lines around March
Branch Lines around Midhurst
Branch Line to Minehead
Branch Line to Moretonhampstead
Branch Lines to Newport (IOW)
Branch Line to Padstow
Branch Lines around Plymouth
Branch Lines to Seaton and Sidmouth
Branch Line to Selsey
Branch Lines around Sheerness
Branch Line to Shrewsbury
Branch Line to Swanage *updated*
Branch Line to Tenterden
Branch Lines to Torrington
Branch Lines to Tunbridge Wells
Branch Line to Upwell
Branch Lines of West London
Branch Lines around Weymouth
Branch Lines around Wisbech

NARROW GAUGE BRANCH LINES
Branch Line to Lynton
Branch Lines around Portmadoc 1923-46
Branch Lines around Porthmadog 1954-94
Branch Line to Southwold
Kent Narrow Gauge
Two-Foot Gauge Survivors
Romneyrail
Southern France Narrow Gauge
Vivarais Narrow Gauge

SOUTH COAST RAILWAYS
Ashford to Dover
Bournemouth to Weymouth
Brighton to Eastbourne
Brighton to Worthing
Dover to Ramsgate
Eastbourne to Hastings
Hastings to Ashford
Portsmouth to Southampton
Southampton to Bournemouth

SOUTHERN MAIN LINES
Basingstoke to Salisbury
Bromley South to Rochester
Crawley to Littlehampton
Dartford to Sittingbourne
East Croydon to Three Bridges
Epsom to Horsham
Exeter to Barnstaple

Exeter to Tavistock
Faversham to Dover
London Bridge to East Croydon
Orpington to Tonbridge
Tonbridge to Hastings
Salisbury to Yeovil
Swanley to Ashford
Tavistock to Plymouth
Victoria to East Croydon
Waterloo to Windsor
Waterloo to Woking
Woking to Portsmouth
Woking to Southampton
Yeovil to Exeter

EASTERN MAIN LINES
Fenchurch Street to Barking
Ipswich to Saxmundham
Liverpool Street to Ilford

WESTERN MAIN LINES
Ealing to Slough
Exeter to Newton Abbot
Paddington to Ealing

COUNTRY RAILWAY ROUTES
Andover to Southampton
Bath Green Park to Bristol
Bath to Evercreech Junction
Bournemouth to Evercreech Jn.
Cheltenham to Andover
Croydon to East Grinstead
Didcot to Winchester
East Kent Light Railway
Fareham to Salisbury
Frome to Bristol
Guildford to Redhill
Porthmadog to Blaenau
Reading to Basingstoke
Reading to Guildford
Redhill to Ashford
Salisbury to Westbury
Stratford upon Avon to Cheltenham
Strood to Paddock Wood
Taunton to Barnstaple
Wenford Bridge to Fowey
Westbury to Bath
Woking to Alton
Yeovil to Dorchester

GREAT RAILWAY ERAS
Ashford from Steam to Eurostar
Clapham Junction 50 years of change
Festiniog in the Fifties
Festiniog in the Sixties
Isle of Wight Lines 50 years of change
Railways to Victory 1944-46
SECR Centenary album
Talyllyn 50 years of change
Yeovil 50 years of change

LONDON SUBURBAN RAILWAYS
Caterham and Tattenham Corner
Charing Cross to Dartford
Clapham Jn. to Beckenham Jn.
East London Line
Finsbury Park to Alexandra Palace
Kingston and Hounslow Loops
Lewisham to Dartford
Lines around Wimbledon
London Bridge to Addiscombe
Mitcham Junction Lines
North London Line
South London Line
West Croydon to Epsom
West London Line

Willesden Junction to Richmond
Wimbledon to Epsom

STEAMING THROUGH
Steaming through Cornwall
Steaming through Kent
Steaming through West Hants
Steaming through West Sussex

TRAMWAY CLASSICS
Aldgate & Stepney Tramways
Barnet & Finchley Tramways
Bath Tramways
Bournemouth & Poole Tramways
Brighton's Tramways
Burton & Ashby Tramways
Camberwell & W.Norwood Tramways
Clapham & Streatham Tramways
Croydon's Tramways
Dover's Tramways
East Ham & West Ham Tramways
Edgware and Willesden Tramways
Eltham & Woolwich Tramways
Embankment & Waterloo Tramways
Enfield & Wood Green Tramways
Exeter & Taunton Tramways
Greenwich & Dartford Tramways
Hammersmith & Hounslow Tramways
Hampstead & Highgate Tramways
Hastings Tramways
Holborn & Finsbury Tramways
Ilford & Barking Tramways
Kingston & Wimbledon Tramways
Lewisham & Catford Tramways
Liverpool Tramways 1. Eastern Routes
Liverpool Tramways 2. Southern Routes
Liverpool Tramways 3. Northern Routes
Maidstone & Chatham Tramways
North Kent Tramways
Norwich Tramways
Portsmouth's Tramways
Reading Tramways
Seaton & Eastbourne Tramways
Shepherds Bush & Uxbridge Tramway
Southampton Tramways
Southend-on-sea Tramways
Southwark & Deptford Tramways
Stamford Hill Tramways
Twickenham & Kingston Tramways
Victoria & Lambeth Tramways
Waltham Cross & Edmonton Tramway
Walthamstow & Leyton Tramways
Wandsworth & Battersea Tramways

TROLLEYBUS CLASSICS
Croydon Trolleybuses
Bournemouth Trolleybuses
Hastings Trolleybuses
Maidstone Trolleybuses
Reading Trolleybuses
Woolwich & Dartford Trolleybuses

WATERWAY ALBUMS
Kent and East Sussex Waterways
London to Portsmouth Waterway
West Sussex Waterways

MILITARY BOOKS
Battle over Portsmouth
Battle over Sussex 1940
Blitz over Sussex 1941-42
Bombers over Sussex 1943-45
Bognor at War
Military Defence of West Sussex
Secret Sussex Resistance
Sussex Home Guard

OTHER RAILWAY BOOKS
Garraway Father & Son
Index to all Middleton Press stations
Industrial Railways of the South-East
South Eastern & Chatham Railways
London Chatham & Dover Railway
War on the Line (SR 1939-45)